British Museum Objects in Focus

The Warren Cup
Dyfri Williams

THE BRITISH MUSEUM PRESS

First published in 2006 by
The British Museum Press
A division of The British Museum
Company Ltd
38 Russell Square
London WC1B 3QQ

britishmuseum.org/publishing

Reprinted 2012, 2014

A catalogue record for this book is available from the British Library

ISBN 978-0-7141-2260-1

Designed by Esterson Associates
Typeset in Miller and
Akzidenz-Grotesque
Printed and bound in China
by C&C Offset

The papers used by The British Museum Press are recyclable products and the manufacturing processes are expected to conform to the environmental regulations of the country of origin.

Acknowledgements
For the photographs of the objects in the British Museum I am very grateful to Ivor Kerslake and P.E. Nichols. For providing photographs of pieces in their own private collections I am much indebted to George Ortiz and Shelby White. For help in securing photographs from other museums and collections I offer thanks in particular to Bodil Bundgaard Rasmussen, Daniel Roger and Anne Spike. To my editor, Laura Lappin, I owe special gratitude for her sympathetic assistance. Finally, many other friends and colleagues have helped in a variety of ways. I should like to mention in particular Robert Guy, Claude Hankes-Drielsma, Catherine Johns, Neil MacGregor, Korinna Pilafidis-Williams, Paul Roberts, David Sox, Alexandra Villing, Susan Walker, Frank Wascheck and, most especially, Susan and Peter Woodford – a ghost's return.

Contents

Chapter One
Introduction

1 Cartoon by Nick Newman for *The Sunday Times*, 9 May 1999.

The acquisition of the silver Warren Cup in 1999 caused something of a stir when it was announced to the press on account of its price (£1.8 million) and its challengingly explicit homoerotic scenes. It was prominently illustrated in all the major daily newspapers, and the reporting varied between the crudely predictable and the much more thoughtful. It was the subject of cartoons (fig. 1) and even featured in the television quiz programme *Have I got News for You.*

The Warren Cup is, in fact, a remarkably important masterpiece of Roman art, created early in the first century AD, which was for too long condemned as a result of its subject matter to an undeserved obscurity. Its scenes reflect the mores of the time and society in which it was created. As such, it is a precious means for us to reach back and understand something of that time and its peoples, while at the same time requiring us to think about our own society and our sexual protocols. One of the British Museum's great tasks is to help visitors understand the many and different cultures of the world. It is perhaps rare that an ancient object should challenge us so directly and explicitly across the centuries, as the Warren Cup does, and this, along with its superb quality, is what makes it so special. Indeed, it has as a result an extraordinary history to tell, both ancient and modern, one that this small book endeavours to explore.

The cup's purchase was made possible by the understanding and generosity of a number of public bodies, especially the Heritage Lottery Fund and the National Art Collections Fund, and several private individuals, all members of the international group of supporters of the Greek and Roman Department, the Caryatids. These pages are offered by way of thanks.

Chapter Two
The Warren Cup

2 *Opposite* The Warren Cup: front view of a man and youth.

3 *Above* The Warren Cup: the inner silver liner.

The Warren Cup is 11 cm high and made of silver that is roughly 95 per cent pure, with a little copper, and small traces of gold and lead. This alloy is perfectly consistent with other known ancient Roman silver vessels, while the corrosion products that remain in the cracks even after both its twentieth-century cleanings prove its antiquity. When created in the early first century AD the cup consisted of five parts. There is a thin-walled bowl with high relief scenes, raised by hammering from inside (*repoussé*), and given further definition and detail by careful chasing from outside. In addition, there is an inner liner of silver, twice as thick as the bowl, with a solid, projecting rim hammered out in one piece with the liner (fig. 3). The repoussé work on the bowl required extraordinary skill, and the resulting thinness and fragility of the wall necessitated the inner bowl for strengthening purposes, and to facilitate cleaning after use.

Later relief bowls from the second half of the first century AD tend to be made from much thicker silver and do not require such a liner – indeed, they are often cast. The Warren Cup originally had a pair of vertical handles that rose, ear-like, from simple palmettes attached low on the wall of the cup between the two scenes, to be soldered on to the top of the rim, thus holding decorated bowl and plain liner together (cf. fig. 18). It was, therefore, strictly speaking in archaeological terms, a *kantharos*. Finally, there is an elaborately profiled foot, which was separately cast, turned and soldered to the base.

The decoration of the cup is almost entirely concentrated on the human figures, there being only a very simple floral calyx of six sepals at the base of the bowl from which the cup seems to blossom. There are two figured scenes in low relief, both set against a background created by a large textile hung over a cord or pole, which would also have been framed by the simple handles. On either side two males

4 *Opposite* The Warren Cup: back view of a youth and boy.

5 *Right* The Warren Cup: side view showing an area for a vertical handle between the scenes.

6 *Below* The Warren Cup: side view showing a slave at the door and an area for a vertical handle between the scenes.

7 *Opposite* The Warren Cup: detail of the front showing the man and youth.

8 *Right* The Warren Cup: detail of the front showing a slave at the door.

share a mattress and are shown in a sexual act. The age and status of all the figures are very carefully delineated. The front is defined by the senior, bearded figure and the presence on the right of an open door (figs 2 and 7–8). The bearded figure wears a myrtle wreath tied at the back with a ribbon, while his companion is a beardless youth and has no wreath. The scene is further enriched by an open chest on the extreme left, on the edge of which rests a complex lyre or *lyra* with eleven strings, framed by the lid behind it. On the right a slave, short-haired and wearing an unbelted, sleeved tunic, somewhat gingerly opens one leaf of a double wooden door. Whether the slave's appearance is voyeuristic or he is simply responding to a call for 'room service', the movement seems to have caught the attention of the youth. On the other side of the cup (figs 4 and 9), the older figure is this time a beardless youth, similarly crowned with a myrtle wreath tied with a ribbon, while his companion is just a boy. On the extreme left is an open chest with a lock: more textiles decoratively spill out of it. Up on the extreme right of the scene, a pair of pipes (*auloi* in ancient Greek) is suspended over the background textile by means of a cord.

On the front (fig. 7) the older figure reclines on his back, his legs spread slightly, bent up and crossed below the knees, his back propped against a large folded cushion with a fringed seam, and his head turned to his right, chin obscured by his right shoulder. The youth has eased himself on to the lap of his older partner with the aid of a strap that appears to hang from the pole supporting the curtain-like background (such straps are to be seen on some other representations of lovemaking in both Greek and Roman art). A plain *chlamys* or cloak envelops the youth's left arm and passes over his right thigh to cascade onto the man's knees and right shin. The man's right hand disappears under the cloak and is perhaps to be thought of as holding the youth's right hip as he guides his entry and encourages further movements; the youth gently lays his hand on the man's wrist. The presence of the cloak recalls the metaphor used by the ancient Greek poet Asklepiades – 'when lovers are hidden by one cloak'. The overall effect of the scene is one of gentle, restrained pleasure – civilized and calm – and of understanding and experience.

On the other side of the cup (fig. 9) the difference in size between the two figures is more obvious and the boy is almost cradled by the youth. The youth's upper body is frontal, his head turned down to the left in concentration. His right hand and arm support the boy's right leg as he lifts it up to make room for his own right leg and to enable entry. He is essentially in a kneeling position, both his feet visible to the far left, toes downward. The boy lies on his side, his right leg trapped below the youth. He rests his right elbow on the cushion in front of him. A *chlamys* or cloak is shown on the left shoulder of the youth; it may be the same garment that passes over the boy's left shoulder and falls over the cushion. Two tucks of this garment seem to be caught between the boy's chest and his forearm. His right hand is clasped and we see a left thumb from a second hand. If this were his own hand, one would see it perhaps as a hint at his pain or discomfort, but it seems that this second thumb is larger than the other. This allows us to read it as the youth's, and so part of a very supportive and intimate gesture, which counteracts the way in which their heads are turned in opposite directions. As on the front of the cup, there is an air of tender calm and concentration, this time combined perhaps with a certain sense of inexperience engendered by the ages of the lovers.

Two details of the hair of these figures on the back should be noted here. The boy has an extra long lock of hair that emanates from the crown of his head and falls in a thick multiple wavy strand down onto his spine. The elder youth has a similar lock, but differently treated. It has been braided and lies flat along the crown of his head: it is clearly visible just above the regular contour of his skull and has slight, chased markings cut into the very low relief to indicate its braiding.

The subtlety of the relief work is remarkable, achieving as it does both the convincing representation of complex poses and the sense of muscles and bones beneath the flesh, ranging from the powerfully muscled man to the soft, unformed delicacy of the boy's body. The representation of the two furniture chests is very ambitious, for both are seen in three-quarter view, causing the *lyra* also to be shown slightly turned out of a fully frontal view. The treatment of the drapery is stylized but very careful, and by means of shallow waves and dimples provides a real sense of thickness and weight without distracting from the figures. The absence of subsidiary ornamentation at the rim or in the neighbourhood of the now missing handles tends to focus the attention all the more on the figures themselves.

It is very likely that some details of these scenes were originally gilded, including the drapery, the furniture, the musical instruments and the leaves that form the wreaths worn by the two main figures. This gilding is now lost as a result of wear. The cup also suffered some damage when the thin wall of the bottom of the bowl was compressed in to the foot, causing a slight lean. This seems to have happened during the cup's modern history, not in antiquity, and probably occurred during or soon after its first modern cleaning in the early twentieth century.

9 The Warren Cup: detail
of the back showing the
youth and boy.

Chapter Three
The collector: Ned Warren

The Warren Cup takes its name from Edward Perry Warren, its first modern owner (fig. 10). Ned Warren was born in 1860, the son of a wealthy American paper manufacturer who lived near Boston, Massachusetts. The Warren family could trace its origins back to settlers who arrived aboard the *Arabella* in 1630, but, it has to be said, its members were rather inconspicuous, except perhaps for one who was arrested in 1674 as a witch. The family's fortune was created by Ned's father, Samuel Dennis Warren, who rose from working in a paper-selling firm as an office boy to being the proprietor of his own paper-manufacturing firm.

Samuel Warren married Susan Clark and the couple had six children. The eldest, Josiah, died very young; the others were, in order of birth, Sam Jnr, Henry, Cornelia, Ned and Fiske. It was a determined, clever, religious and idiosyncratic family, but Ned was to be the most unusual. His sister, Cornelia, recalled that when other children played Cowboys and Indians, he ran about in a Roman-style toga. He longed romantically for a 'grand but blighted life' and experimented with various religious denominations. He even used to dress up in a night-gown and pale blue Japanese scarf to read Morning Prayer and Litany to his indulgent mother.

At the age of eight Ned made his first trip to Europe and it clearly had a great impact on him. He candidly admits in a fragment of an autobiography which he began in the last years of his life that on this trip he was left alone, at his own insistence, in the sculpture galleries, while the rest of his family went to see the pictures, and that his interest 'was not wholly artistic'. Ned also admits to having had crushes on boys at school and having even written a poem comparing one of them to the Roman emperor Hadrian's favourite youth, Antinous.

In 1879 Ned went to Harvard. There he suffered by comparison with his sporty elder brother, Sam, and as

11 Ned Warren (left) and John Marshall at Lewes House: they called each other 'puppy'.

a result was not very happy. His fascination with religion continued, but nothing satisfied a deeper need that he was beginning to recognize, the need for a close and lasting friendship with another young man. By the end of his time at Harvard it is clear that this struggle to reconcile his religious convictions with his homosexual feelings finally reached a climax. He decided to give up both religion and Boston.

Oxford, the home of the Aesthetic Movement, beckoned and in 1884, at the age of twenty-five, he persuaded his parents to let him move there to study Classics. Ned met John Marshall in his first year at New College: Marshall was already in his third year, although Ned was two years older. Marshall was a bright Liverpudlian and the two were to become very close (fig. 11). Ned's first year went well and he took a First in Moderations. Marshall took a First in Greats the following summer, but by then Ned's eyesight had begun to weaken and his studies as a result had started to suffer, so that when he went down in 1888 he had only achieved a Pass degree.

Marshall had been destined in the eyes of his parents to go into the Church, but after finishing his degree he turned his back on such a future. In the summer of 1887 Ned was in Naples, probably with Marshall, and there he wrote his

first essay on the subject of love, 'A Tale of Pausanian Love'.
It is essentially an autobiography disguised as a novella,
with Ned as the narrator and Marshall the other chief
character. Ned included the name of Pausanias in his title
because of the *encomium* on Heavenly Love (Aphrodite
Ourania) delivered by Pausanias in Plato's *Symposium*.
Aphrodite Ourania was thought to inspire love between
males, and was held both to be stronger and more
intelligent than Common Love (Aphrodite Pandemos),
and to be spiritual rather than physical. It seems clear,
therefore, that at Oxford Warren began to sublimate his
feelings by intellectualizing them. Nevertheless, he yearned
for a like-minded friend with whom to share his life and
work, an *alter ego*, as he thought of him.

The Warrens had been a very wealthy family since about
1870, although Ned had never shown this at Oxford. When
his father died in May 1888 he left a family trust of $1.9
million. By late 1889 Ned had persuaded Marshall to come
and live with him and serve as his secretary. After searching
for a suitable house Warren eventually hit upon Lewes
House in Lewes, East Sussex, the lease of which he took
in 1890 (fig. 12).

Warren's aim was to begin collecting Classical antiquities,
and Marshall proved a very capable ally. Their first major

outing was to the sale in Paris in May 1892 of a superb collection of vases formed by the Belgian connoisseur, Adolphe van Branteghem. Despite the presence of the major museums, great private collectors, such as the Danish brewer Carl Jacobsen, and powerful dealers such as Count Michel Tyszkiewicz, Warren and Marshall came away with a huge haul including the prize of the whole sale, a red-figured cup signed by the great potter, Euphronios. They were instantly major players.

The driving force behind the partnership was clearly Warren. He it was who had first conceived of collecting Classical antiquities, an idea that combined his love for Classical art with a passion for collecting that he probably inherited from his mother. He also quickly realized the need for a whole variety of contacts to help secure antiquities, ranging from well-established local dealers to contacts in the field, so to speak. For some ten years, until about 1902, life was full of winter trips to the Mediterranean to purchase the local peasants' winter harvest of antiquities. These trips were followed by quieter periods at Lewes House, sorting, mending and cataloguing their finds. Gradually the staff at Lewes House grew, as Warren drew in more friends and helpers. This was to cause many internal tensions, but Warren was always the one to hold the group together and keep up the momentum.

The initial burst of collecting went on for more than two years, but it could not continue forever, for the financial outlay was enormous. Indeed, Warren had perhaps always intended that the material should go to America, for he wrote: 'We are doing the work most needed of all works, supplying eventually the terrible gap that exists on this new continent, the absence of that which delights the eye and rests the soul.' Warren's family had close associations with the Museum of Fine Arts in Boston, for his elder brother Sam was on the Board of Trustees, like his father before him. At first Ned began by giving a few pieces to the museum and putting others on loan, but in 1894 he opened financial negotiations with the museum. It claimed poverty, but then suddenly received two massive bequests and, following a visit by the curator, Edward Robinson, to Lewes

13 The Chios Head, Hellenistic marble head of Aphrodite, from Chios (Museum of Fine Arts, Boston).

House, the astonishing opportunity that was being offered was finally appreciated. There then followed eight years of immense activity and great enjoyment, punctuated by negotiations with Boston over what Warren and Marshall called their almost yearly 'Sendings'.

The list of great works of Classical art that Warren sent to Boston during these years is nothing short of miraculous. From it one might select an extraordinarily delicate head with a dreamy, almost mystic quality, purchased by Marshall on the island of Chios in 1900 (fig. 13). In this adventure he had been aided by some of Warren's other young men from Lewes House: Matthew Stewart Prichard helped with the negotiations on Chios and John Fothergill

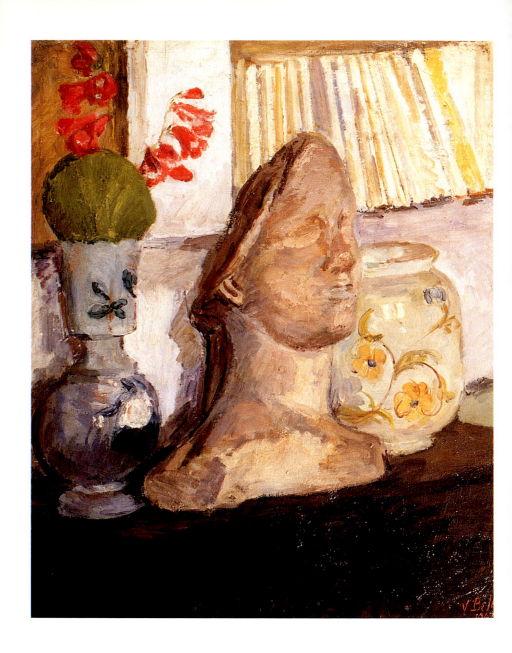

smuggled it out of Greece wrapped in a blanket. Marshall was immensely taken with the head and felt that it had to be the work of the great sculptor Praxiteles, writing a long article for the leading German periodical in an attempt to argue the point. It was also greatly admired by the sculptor Auguste Rodin, who visited Lewes House in 1903. He subsequently not only wrote about the head in a prominent French magazine, but even tried to persuade first Warren and then Marshall to exchange it for some of his own sculptures.

This contact with Rodin was only one of the connections that existed between Warren's set at Lewes House and other artistic and literary circles. In 1898 Warren was persuaded to put up money to found the Carfax Gallery in London, the brainchild of John Fothergill. An early collaborator in this venture was William Rothenstein, another friend of Warren's; it was he who introduced Warren to Rodin. In 1903 Roger Fry had his first very successful one-man show at the Carfax. We know that Fry was a good friend, who stayed at Lewes House many times, sometimes with his family when Warren and Marshall were away. It was probably on one of these visits, in 1908, that he made the watercolour of Lewes House (see fig. 12). Fry was part of the Bloomsbury Group, and Vanessa Bell and Duncan Grant, two of its other members, spent time in Sussex in the neighbourhood of Firle not far from Lewes. In 1911 Duncan Grant had exhibited a painting at the Carfax Gallery and later had his first one-man show there. It is perhaps not surprising, therefore, to find that he acquired a cast of Warren's Chios Head that still survives at Charleston, and that Vanessa Bell included it in two of her later still-life paintings (fig. 14).

1902 was to be a watershed, for the Boston Museum had begun a grandiose building programme that eventually caused the funding of purchases from Warren to cease. It must have been particularly galling that Boston did this just when Marshall and Warren had the market so completely in their hands that Arthur Murray of the British Museum could say 'there is nothing to get nowadays, since Warren and Marshall are always on the spot first'. Warren was to go on talking of rounding off the Boston collection, but new purchases tended to be for himself.

The changes at Boston also led to the resignation of Edward Robinson. He moved on to the Metropolitan Museum in New York, where almost his first act was to invite Marshall to be his salaried purchasing agent. Warren accepted Marshall's independent step, but Warren and Marshall were drifting apart, and what had always been a relationship fraught with deep insecurities, especially on Marshall's side, eventually collapsed, as Marshall married Warren's cousin, Mary Bliss.

Other changes in Warren's life also go back to these years when, after the death of his mother in 1901, he began to see more clearly how his elder brother Sam had manipulated the family trust and cheated Ned and his other siblings out of huge sums of money. The bitter exchanges split the family apart. As he slowed down the purchasing, Ned spent more time writing, and this period of literary activity culminated in 1903 in the completion of a volume of poems called *Itamos*, which contain much passion and much scholarship (later enlarged and published as *The Wild Rose*). During this period Ned corresponded with Goldsworthy Lowes Dickinson, who was a very close friend of Roger Fry and whose Cambridge set later included E.M. Forster. Forster was to write in 1913 his own self-suppressed novel of homosexual love, *Maurice* (only published posthumously in 1970).

It was probably in 1908 that Warren first met J.D. Beazley, the young Oxford scholar who was at that time leaving behind the writing of poetry and breaking new ground in the study of the painters of Athenian vases. Jack Beazley and Ned Warren became very close. Beazley seems to have helped by attributing Warren's vases; Warren supported Beazley's work on the vases in America. Indeed, Beazley dedicated his first book to the pair in 1918 and went on, in 1920, to publish Warren's great collection of engraved gems that was later sold to Boston. It is from Beazley, too, that a number of pieces of information about the Warren Cup have come down to us, as we shall see later.

In 1910, as Warren turned fifty, his elder brother, Sam, unable to cope with the court-case that Ned eventually set in motion and with all that began to be revealed, committed suicide. Ned's family blamed him for this tragedy and the wounds never properly healed. One outcome, however, was the final solution of all the problems with the family trust, which led to Ned's sudden increase in spending power.

In 1911 we hear, rather mysteriously, from Osbert Burdett and E.H. Goddard, Warren's official biographers, of one special object that attracted Ned's attention and required his presence in Rome. The journey at first seemed tiresome to Ned, but turned out to be a pleasant interlude that brought back many memories of earlier expeditions. On his way he visited Rodin in Paris; in Rome he took the opportunity of seeing many old friends, including the infamous Oscar Browning of the Cambridge set, and all the dealers. Burdett and Goddard do not tell us what the special object was, but they say that it cost £2,000 – a huge sum for those days – and that it was still unsold at the time of writing (1936). There is only one object that could have cost such a sum, that would have drawn Warren all the way across Europe to secure it and that remained unsold long after his death: the silver cup with homoerotic scenes.

Soon after this acquisition, Warren began work on what he called his 'Magnum Opus', *A Defence of Uranian Love* (a cult of Uranism had been developed by the Austrian Karl Heinrich Ulrichs in the early 1860s). Ned's is an extraordinary work, a sort of final 'testament' that complements his earlier lyric poems. It presents a complete theory that prefers a Greek masculine ideal, based on aristocracy, nobility and the secondary position of women, to a Christian feminine ideal that includes democracy, purity and the equality of the sexes. It is in many ways a very personal summation of how a remarkable, scholarly aesthete came to terms with his own sexuality, and how he learned to accept his ageing through a belief in the education that an older lover can give to a younger. But there is much that reveals the pain that Ned must have suffered and the strict discipline of restraint that he imposed on himself, a discipline that required of the elder partner – the *erastes* ('lover') of the Greek pattern – 'the power to lack, and give without return'. The elder *erastes*

should also help the younger *eromenos* ('beloved') to a
proper marriage, should he not wish to remain a Uranian.
Warren thus envisaged a series of fleeting attachments
repeated in maturity, governed by discipline, and a
progression for the likes of himself from the love for many
beauties to the Platonic Absolute, becoming 'father, friend,
remembrancer, guard – [and] if the best be reached, saint'.

Ned lived by this theory of morals, and only with its help
can one begin to understand his aims and actions. The book
and the earlier poems illuminate life at Lewes House – the
rather monastic atmosphere, with meals served on a huge
oak table flanked by church benches and overlooked by
Lucas Cranach's *Adam and Eve* (fig. 15); the daily ritual of
reading, exercise (riding his Arab stallions or playing bowls
on the lawn) and communal meals; the music, provided
sometimes by Ned himself, who played the clavichord
beautifully; and the study of the collection. Beazley was
to sum up Lewes House with the words 'Within, calm,
work, a mine of treasures, a shrine of friendship, a spirit
of tranquil beauty'.

Ned's inner sanctum was his private study over the
stables, well away from the rest of the house. He called it
'Thebes', after ancient Thebes where the pederastic ideal
was openly fostered, as exemplified by the 'Sacred Band'
of the Theban army, in which the love between *erastes* and
eromenos bound the warriors in honour unto death. It was
here that he kept his more precious antiquities, under lock
and key (a gold key that he kept round his neck). As he sat
there writing his Magnum Opus, he may well have
contemplated his new silver cup.

Ned was clearly proud of this acquisition, and showed
it to friends and colleagues alike. Indeed, Dietrich von
Bothmer recalls Beazley telling him that Ned Warren
and his friends at Lewes House referred to it as the 'Holy
Grail'. In 1921 Ned allowed photographs of it to be used as
the first item in Gaston Vorberg's collection of illustrations
of ancient erotica. However, he never attempted to sell it,
although he did have a copy made that passed to Beazley,
who was in turn to give it to the Ashmolean Museum
in 1966.

When Ned Warren died in 1928, aged sixty-eight, only nine months after John Marshall, his estate, most of which he left to his last secretary, Harold Thomas, contained paintings by Filippino Lippi (now in Cleveland) and Lucas Cranach (see fig. 15, now in the Courtauld Institute, London), as well as medieval and modern sculptures, and a large collection of early silver. Two important pieces in this bequest were to have remarkably parallel fates, charting the history of society's reactions to sex: the famous marble sculpture known as the *The Kiss*, which Warren had commissioned from Rodin in 1900, and the Roman silver cup with homoerotic scenes, the Warren Cup.

The commissioning of *The Kiss* (fig. 16) followed a visit by Warren to Paris, where he had been encouraged by the artist William Rothenstein to seek out Rodin's *Le Baiser*, then on show. Warren and Rodin made a contract for a second version of the sculpture, *The Kiss*, as it was to be known: the cost was to be £1,000. It was to be carved from Pentelic marble; the male genitals were to be fully carved (unlike *Le Baiser*); and the work was to be finished in eighteen months. Rodin, however, took four years. After a successful showing in London in 1906 *The Kiss* went to Lewes House where it stayed for some eight years, before it was placed in the Assembly Room at Lewes as a potential gift to the town. The local councillors, however, did not like it – it was 'too big and too nude'. Later Warren offered it to Boston, but there it was refused as being 'too fleshy'. Immediately after Warren's death, Harold W. Parsons, the last of Warren's companions, who was then European adviser for the Cleveland Museum of Art, was keen to secure some of the collection for commissioned sale in America and wrote to Harry Thomas in alarm when he heard that Thomas was putting everything up for sale locally: 'the silver bowl will be less easy; you should bide your time with that piece. Don't be stampeded into selling... [this] or the big Rodin group, for if you are patient you will get big prices, but one has to negotiate.' Thomas ignored this advice and *The Kiss* did not sell. In due course, just before the Second World War, it was put on loan in the Tate Gallery. Nevertheless, in late 1952, shortly before Thomas

16 *The Kiss*, Pentelic marble by Auguste Rodin, 1904, commissioned by Ned Warren; seen here at Lewes House (now Tate Modern).

died, Parsons tried for another commissioned sale by offering it to Kansas City, only to be told that 'it would never do'. It was left, in the end, to Sir John Rothenstein, son of the artist William Rothenstein, one of Warren's close friends, to mount a public appeal to raise the £7,500 needed for *The Kiss* to stay in the Tate.

The silver cup's similar challenge to social norms began with Thomas's first attempt to sell it at the auction of the contents of Lewes House in October 1929. Harold Parsons had, as we have seen, warned of the problems surrounding any such attempt, and it did not sell (it was not even explicitly described in the sale catalogue). Thereafter, perhaps at Parsons' suggestion, Thomas sent it off to be cleaned. Nevertheless, it was to stay with Thomas until the last years of his life, hidden away in the attic. In November 1952 Parsons was again to try to take the sale of the cup in hand and attempted to interest the New York collector Walter Baker in it. Baker, however, hesitated – Bothmer remarked in a letter to Beazley at the time 'I think he is afraid of what his wife will say'. Then suddenly in February of the next year the cup arrived quite unexpectedly in New York, consigned by Thomas to Walter Baker. This suggests that Parsons, clearly the most unscrupulous of Warren's friends, had been trying to earn a commission on the sale of the cup again, rather against Thomas's wishes. However, when the cup was inspected by a US Customs official of Italian origin and Catholic faith, its subject was at once observed and the box resealed pending a decision from Washington whether to allow the import of pornography. The wheels of officialdom ground slowly and the cup, having been refused entry, was not returned to England until October of the following year, by which time Harry Thomas had died.

Upon its return, it was quickly sold off by Thomas's widow to John K. Hewett, the leading British dealer. Hewett showed it to the then Keeper of the Greek and Roman Department at the British Museum, Denys Haynes. Haynes, realizing its importance but also the problems of the subject matter, decided to show it first to his friend Lord Crawford, an influential Trustee. Lord Crawford, however, felt that, with the Chairman of the Trustees still being the Archbishop of Canterbury, any proposal to purchase the cup would founder immediately. Haynes therefore returned the cup to Hewett. A few years later it was offered to the Fitzwilliam Museum in Cambridge, but its Syndics were no braver. Having failed with public institutions, Hewett next tried the private sector. He offered it first to the British collector Norman Colville, who in customary fashion had it sent to him on approval, sight unseen, but when he had the box opened he was horrified and sent it straight back. It was not until 1966 that Hewett finally sold the Warren Cup to a private collector abroad.

By the mid-1980s perceptions of ancient art and of homosexuality were at last beginning to change and the owner took the bold step of placing the cup on public display in the Antikenmuseum in Basel. In 1992 it was moved to the Metropolitan Museum of Art. Its sudden removal in 1998 and sale to a British private collector gave the British Museum a second chance to offer the cup a permanent home in the public domain.

It is interesting to observe that although as an American Warren caused so many extraordinary antiquities to cross the Atlantic Ocean, the country in which he chose to live for nearly two thirds of his life still holds perhaps the three grandest works of art that he ever collected, the Courtauld's Cranach, the Tate's *The Kiss* and the British Museum's Warren Cup.

17 Pair of silver *kantharoi* with floral decoration inhabited by birds and insects, said to be from Asia Minor (British Museum).

Chapter Four

Roman tableware: silver, glass and pottery

The Warren Cup is a luxury drinking vessel, and as such belongs in the sphere of convivial eating and drinking that formed one of the key social rituals in the Roman world. Such dining or *convivium* ('living together') played an essential role in the bonding of members of the élite with each other and with their dependants. These *convivia* were held in a special room in the house, the *triclinium*, set out to take three large dining couches arranged around a central rectangular space for tables. Each couch could take up to three diners, and women might attend and recline, although there are few representations of citizen women doing so. Wine accompanied the meal throughout. Indeed, the Romans were real wine connoisseurs, distinguishing wines from different regions and even developing the idea of a *grand cru*.

Such *convivia* were opportunities for the display of wealth, whether through the elaborateness of the food and the number of courses – as we read in 'Trimalchio's Dinner', part of Petronius's *Satyricon* – or through the costliness of the service (*ministerium*) from which the guests ate and drank. Roman silverware for the table was divided into two groups by function: eating silver (*argentum escarium*) and drinking silver (*argentum potorium*). Among the former were plates, dishes and bowls of all sizes and shapes, egg-cups, and shakers for salt and pepper, as well as spoons (but no knives, since all was prepared in finger-sized morsels, and no forks, since they had not yet been invented). Among the latter were amphorae, jugs, wine bowls, dippers, strainers and a wide variety of shapes of drinking vessels, especially deep two-handled cups and one-handled mugs.

In the sets, or parts of sets, of drinking silver that have been preserved for us by the eruption of Mt Vesuvius in AD 79 among the house and villa treasures at Pompeii and Boscoreale, we find numerous pairs of drinking cups of various shapes. Even when silver is found in other contexts, such pairs are sometimes still together, as in the hoard from Hockwold in provincial Britannia, perhaps buried in the face of Boudicca's revolt; or the diplomatic gift that was placed in a chieftain's tomb at Hoby in Denmark. When we examine these pairs we find that their subjects or scenes are either virtually identical or in some way complementary. The decoration can be completely floral (figs 17 and 27–8), or centre on animals – as on a pair of *kantharoi* from Boscoreale with storks (fig. 18) – or on some human activity, sometimes rustic, sometimes ritual. The Hoby *skyphoi* (wide-mouthed, two-handled drinking cups) have mythological scenes taken from the Trojan legend: Priam's appeal to Achilles for the release of Hektor's body, and the washing of Philoktetes' wound (fig. 19). Some other cups present contemporary political scenes, such as a pair of elaborate *skyphoi* from the Boscoreale Treasure with representations of the emperor Augustus and his heir Tiberius. In the case of the Warren Cup, therefore, we might reasonably suppose that it was once one of a pair. Indeed, it has been suggested that its mate might have had scenes of men and women making love, but it is also possible that

18 One of a pair of silver *kantharoi* with storks, from Boscoreale, Italy (Musée du Louvre, Paris).

it in fact carried similar scenes to the first, only with slight variations of pose and setting.

The preference for pairs of decorated cups and, it would seem, the occasional trio, with matching or complementary scenes, and the variety of shapes makes one ponder how exactly they might have been used at the *convivium*. Perhaps the answer is to be found in the number of guests on each couch – two probably being the most comfortable arrangement at a private dinner – and the variety of wines or courses on offer. Conversation at such gatherings was an important feature, and the decoration of the cups held by the guests provided a natural topic for discussion and the display of erudition. One can perhaps imagine the scene on the London Chryses *kantharos* (figs 20–21 and 27; of a somewhat different shape to the Warren Cup, its foot and two high-arching handles now missing), together with its lost complementary mate, evoking initial puzzlement, relieved eventually by the host pointing out the subject and recalling a lively performance of Pacuvius's tragedy *Chryses*; or if beaten to that end by a guest, trumping it with the knowledge of an earlier play on the same theme by Sophokles.

Such splendid, decorated drinking vessels were made for use by the wealthy echelons of the middle class; the

20 The Chryses silver *kantharos*, said to be from Asia Minor, showing Iolaos, Iphigeneia and Orestes taking refuge at the altar of Apollo (British Museum).

imperial family seems to have used gold plate (at least from the time of the emperor Tiberius) and sometimes semi-precious stone such as agate. Some may have been 'off the shelf' purchases; but where the iconography was beyond the ordinary, then we are probably right to consider them as special commissions, whether of a private kind, as was surely the case with the Warren Cup, or of a more public nature, as with the imperial *skyphoi* from Boscoreale. The use of spectacular silverware as diplomatic gifts resulted in its wide distribution well beyond the Roman world, from Britain and Denmark in the north to Sudan in the south, and to Pakistan and even China in the east.

The growing demand for silver vessels in the second half of the first century BC led to the employment of craftsmen from all over the old Hellenistic world. Many were Greeks, as is indicated by the signature of the craftsman in between the figures on the two *skyphoi* from Hoby (see fig. 19): 'Cheirisophos made' on one cup in Greek and on the other transliterated into Latin. The name ('skilled with the

21 The Chryses silver *kantharos*, showing Chryseis, Chryses, and Thoas and an attendant (British Museum).

hands') suggests that the maker was a slave or freedman of Greek origin, but working for a Roman clientèle. There were no doubt a number of workshops in Rome itself and there may have been workshops or travelling craftsmen elsewhere throughout the Roman world, including the Hellenized south of Italy and some of the cosmopolitan centres in the eastern Mediterranean. The general uniformity of the style of the more elaborate pieces, however, especially those with figured scenes, suggests that almost without exception they were all created in Rome. Indeed, we can sometimes discover vessels that must have been made in the very same workshop. This is, of course, easy to detect when we are dealing with a pair, such as the *kantharoi* in the British Museum with florals inhabited by birds and insects (see fig. 17); but we may also suggest that the more elaborate, figured *kantharos* from the same find (said to have been in Asia Minor), the Chryses *kantharos*, was made in the same workshop, for it has very similar florals on the lower part of the bowl (see figs 20–21 and 27).

22 Detail of a cameo glass jug ('Auldjo Jug') with florals and birds, from the House of the Faun, Pompeii (British Museum).

The Warren Cup now weighs 359 g. To judge from other examples of the same form and size, it originally probably weighed about 485 g when its handles were still attached, that is about 1½ Roman pounds or 125 silver *denarii* in Roman coinage. Indeed, just such a number of coins were probably handed to the silversmith by the commissioner for melting down to make the object, together with a small amount of gold for the gilding (now lost), perhaps also in coin. An additional sum would also have been negotiated to cover the cost of the time and skill of the craftsman, a sum that may have been between 2 and 5 per cent. The resultant total should then probably be doubled to account for the lost mate. To understand the actual value of this in the first century AD, one might note that 250 *denarii* would have purchased one *iugerum* of land (approximately two thirds of an acre), an unskilled slave, or twenty-five amphorae of the best wine.

Clearly there were also close interconnections between silver vessels and cameo glass vessels at this period, for we find some of the same motifs in both materials. For example, the florals inhabited by little birds on the pair of large silver *kantharoi* in the British Museum (see fig. 17) can be paralleled on a fragmentary cameo glass jug in the British Museum, the so-called Auldjo Jug (fig. 22). Similarly, the scene of a youth and a boy on the Warren Cup also has a parallel on a cameo glass flask in a Swiss private collection, said to come from Spain. On one side of this a male and a female are about to make love (fig. 23, right): she wears a breast band; he kneels as he readies himself to enter from behind. On the other side (fig. 23, left), a youth kneels as he enters a boy, who holds a garland in one hand. Furthermore, a fragment in the British Museum from what was once a superb cameo *skyphos* (fig. 24), made of six layers of coloured glass, follows the form of the scene on the flask in a Swiss collection (but without the garland). Interestingly this extraordinary fragment, found in Rome in the early nineteenth century and given to the Museum by Sir Charles Newton (Keeper of Greek and Roman Antiquities, 1861–86), was hidden away in the so-called 'Museum Secretum' because of its subject matter, only to be registered in the collection in 1956 by a far less repressive generation. One side of the Warren Cup is, in fact, very similar in overall conception, but different in some details to these glass pieces.

One other category of material shows scenes that seem to derive from similar sources as the representations on the silver and cameo glass vessels. This is pottery, in particular the glossy red Italian pottery known as Arretine ware. The finest production of Arretine pottery, with its moulded reliefs, dates to the last quarter of the first century BC and the first decade or two of the first century AD. A couple of fragments match the scene on one of the Hoby cups, while a number of fragments of vessels and moulds from and for a variety of shapes – the products of two different Arretine workshops – repeat the elaborate scene on the London Chryses *kantharos*. Similarly, a series of fragments of vessels and moulds of Arretine pottery match the male lovemaking scene on the cameo glass flask in a Swiss collection and the London six-layered fragment. A good example is that given by Ned Warren to the Museum of Fine Arts in Boston (fig. 25). It originally showed alternating couples of a youth with a boy and a youth with a woman,

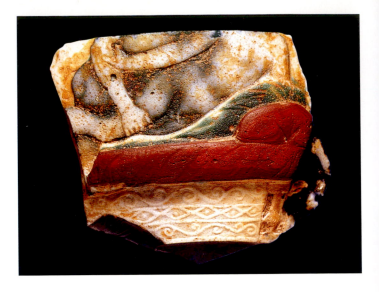

naked but for a breast band. Although the figures can be very similar, there are differences in details and in some poses so the potters cannot have been simply taking casts directly off the silver vessels. Perhaps both potters and silversmiths drew on a common repertoire of images and scenes enjoyed by the educated élite.

Such pottery, although often of high quality, was mass-produced in moulds and consequently far less expensive, not least because of the cheapness of the raw material, clay. Glass similarly relied on cheap materials and, once the technique of glass-blowing had been invented in the second half of the first century BC, the glass-makers were free to experiment with all sorts of shapes and decorative systems and techniques. Cameo glass was one such novel technique developed late in the first century BC that required the careful carving away of the outer layer or layers and thus became a luxury item. Like silver vessels, cameo glass travelled widely, from Spain to Iran, perhaps also as diplomatic gifts. Interestingly, it seems to have been produced over roughly the same period as Arretine pottery, and there may at this time have been considerable rivalry and artistic interchange between craftsmen, whether working in clay, glass or silver.

25 Arretine bowl with scenes of lovemaking (Museum of Fine Arts, Boston).

By the middle of the first century AD the élite were faced with something of a dilemma, one voiced by Trimalchio at his dinner party: 'You may forgive me if I say that personally I prefer glass; glass at least does not smell. If it were not so breakable I should prefer it to gold, as it is so cheap.' Blown-glass vessels were then the norm, many blown into a mould to give relief scenes without the need to cut away a layer of glass. Silver vessels continued to be made, but became heavier as a greater display of wealth was required, and the scenes on them were cast rather than hammered. The specialist Arretine pottery workshops, however, with their laboriously created relief scenes, suddenly came to an end and pottery, though still ubiquitous, became even more mass-produced with workshops throughout the empire.

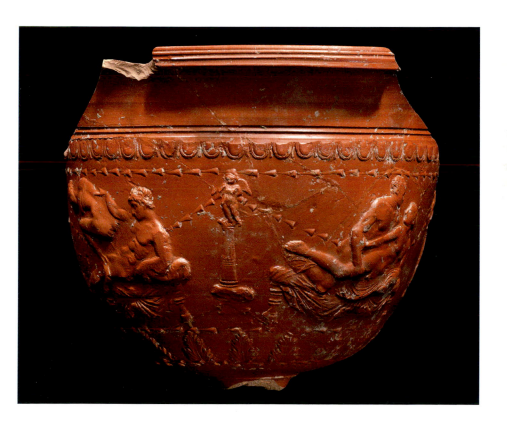

Chapter Five

Date and findspot of the Warren Cup

26 Detail of the Chryses silver *kantharos* (fig. 20), showing Iolaos and Iphigeneia (British Museum).

Most ancient silver vessels have been lost to us because they were melted down, either in antiquity or in later centuries. Sometimes, however, silver was preserved in tombs, in hoards hidden in times of crisis or danger, or very occasionally in contexts sealed by natural disasters. In the case of Roman silver much that has survived was sealed by the eruption of Mt Vesuvius in AD 79, especially the material from the villa at Boscoreale and the House of the Menander at Pompeii. The small quantity of preserved silver vessels, however, makes dating difficult. Even the material preserved by the Vesuvian eruption is problematic, for it is clear that these groups contain material amassed over several generations. Nevertheless, careful study and comparison of decorative style and shape give a certain idea of the development of Roman silver vessels.

Given the close thematic and stylistic connections, it seems likely that pieces such as the British Museum's Chryses *kantharos* (see figs 20–21) or the Hoby *skyphoi* (see fig. 19) were made between the years 15 BC and AD 20 when the Arretine pottery factories were at their height and there was an astonishing flowering of Roman art. Within this period one can perhaps discern a growing spareness in the subsidiary decoration and often a reduction in the height of the relief work as we move from the early Augustan pieces to the later ones. An example of the earlier pieces with high-relief extravaganzas of olive, vine or ivy is a piece with vine leaves in the British Museum (fig. 27; its mate is in the Naples Museum). The Boscoreale cups with their crowded, political scenes are still rendered in high relief, and probably to be dated to soon after 8 BC, the date of Tiberius's first triumph. The later Augustan works may be represented by the low relief florals of the London *kantharoi* (see fig 17 and 28), which should date well after the completion of Augustus's *Ara Pacis* (Altar of Peace) with its wonderful floral panels similarly inhabited by tiny creatures: it was dedicated in 9 BC. The Hoby skyphoi (see fig. 19), with their lower relief figures and more restrained, mythological scenes, have been dated on the basis of the owner inscriptions underneath the feet to the first decade or so of the first century AD. The Warren Cup seems to match this late Augustan phase and one may suppose that it too belongs late in Augustus's reign or very early in that of his successor Tiberius (AD 14–37). Indeed, the style of the relief scenes is so close to that on the Hoby *skyphoi* that one is much tempted to wonder if they might not have been made by the very same master silversmith, the Greek Cheirisophos. Finally, the shape of the foot of the Warren Cup is most closely paralleled on a *kantharos* found in a hoard of silver at Buner in the North West Frontier Province of Pakistan: it is decorated with centaurs carrying off Lapith women also in a low relief style that recalls the Hoby and Warren vessels.

If, then, we may date the Warren Cup perhaps to the years between AD 5 and 15, we may go on to begin to ask how long

28 Detail of a silver *kantharos* (fig. 17) with floral decoration inhabited by birds and insects (British Museum).

it remained in its owner's or owners' possession, for it is clearly heavily worn as a result of cleaning and handling. Silver vessels required regular cleaning and some wealthy households kept slaves whose duties were solely to clean the silver. One might also add to the equation both the reports in our literary sources of inherited silver (including Trimalchio who mentions a piece that he inherited from his patron, a bowl showing the Trojan Horse) and the occasional occurrence of several owners' names scratched on a vessel. Bearing such factors in mind, we can easily imagine that the Warren Cup remained in use over a couple of generations.

What, then, of the findspot of the Warren Cup – its final ancient context? This had been said, rather vaguely, to be in Syria or Palestine, but David Sox's discovery of a list made in 1938 for Harry Thomas of Warren's objects that had not sold at the auction of the contents of Lewes House in 1929 following Warren's death has brought new precision. The list contains not only a clear description of the silver cup, but also a precise statement as to its reported findspot:

'Said to have been found at Bittir, six miles from Jerusalem, 20 feet underground.' In addition, Ned's friend, J.D. Beazley, preserved a report that the cup had been found with coins of the emperor Claudius (AD 41–54). Ned Warren was always very careful to preserve what reliable information he could elicit from a dealer as to the find context of any piece he bought. As a result, we may give a good deal of credence to the report of the discovery of the Warren Cup near Jerusalem. We do not know for certain who the dealer was that sold Warren the cup in 1911, but there is every likelihood that it was Ludwig Pollak, who lived in Rome and had very good connections with Palestine and the Jerusalem area in particular, ever since his extended trip there in 1900. Finally, it seems that the find context of the cup was more probably that of a hoard hidden in a time of private or public danger, either during or after Claudius's reign, than a domestic or funerary one.

How did such an extraordinary silver cup come to be in Judaea and to be hidden there? The most likely scenario, especially when one bears in mind the fact that it is heavily worn (perhaps representing a couple of generations of ownership), is that it was in the face of the growing unrest that led to the first Jewish Revolt (AD 66–74). The hiding spot may well have been a cave in one of the escarpments typical of the area. Bittir has long been identified as the ancient Bethther, where Bar Kochba made his final stand against the Roman legions in AD 135, when Jewish resistance was finally and brutally crushed. It is unlikely, however, that Bethther included in its population a rich Roman or Greek, or even that its headman was strongly Romanized or Hellenized. Rather, one might imagine that the cup was hidden by a Roman (or a Greek) fleeing Jerusalem along the Roman road that headed west past the town, terrified at the wave of violence that culminated in the complete take-over of the city by the Jews in August AD 66. Unless, of course, the damaged state of the cup and its apparent solitariness might indicate that it was actually part of the haul of one of the lawless gangs of *sicarii* (cut-throats) that at that time lay in ambush on such roads.

Judaea had been a land torn by internal strife, both

29 Marble portrait of the Roman emperor Vespasian (AD 69–79), excavated at Carthage (British Museum).

economic and religious, for many years. In AD 6 it was made into a Roman province, but Jerusalem was left rather to look after itself under Augustus's tactful rule. Things began to go badly wrong, however, under Tiberius. Matters went from bad to worse under a series of incompetent procurators, until in AD 66 the small Roman garrison was massacred. This caused Nero to put the tried and trusted soldier, Vespasian (fig. 29), in charge of an expeditionary force. Vespasian started well, but upon the death of Nero in AD 68 he returned to Rome, subsequently to take over the empire himself, leaving his son Titus to finish the destruction of Jerusalem that we now know so well from the reliefs on his triumphal arch in Rome.

It is extraordinary to imagine that the Warren Cup might have been taken to Judaea by a wealthy Roman official of some sort, that it was there during the years in which Pontius Pilate was Governor of the province (AD 26–37), and that its owner could have witnessed the various religious crises of Pilate's administration and those leading up to the fall of Jerusalem.

Chapter Six
Sex and society: Greeks and Romans

Let us look now at the scenes on the Warren Cup once again
and see if we can learn more about the people represented
in them, and thus something of how the cup might have
been viewed by its owner or owners.

The indications of the physical setting seem to point in
two different directions. The use of heavy textiles hung from
poles to mark off private space and the mattresses seemingly
without couches (although on the Arretine vases and the
glass vessels we see couches) might suggest an outdoor
setting. The door, however, points to the interior of a room,
as perhaps do the chests of clothes – a bedroom it would
seem. Perhaps the craftsman has in mind a garden scene
on a summer's evening, the door being that to one of the
rooms off the garden or colonnade. The slave peeping round
the door (see fig. 8) is the youngest figure on the cup and his
short-cropped hair and unbelted tunic indicate his status,
but his function is unclear since he carries nothing. In fact,
he doubles as you, the viewer, whether ancient or modern,
and looks at the erotic scene before him as you look at the
cup, a transgressive voyeur who views an otherwise private
sexual play that cannot be joined.

On the front of the cup (fig. 30) the older lover has a
short beard. This is very un-Roman for the first century AD
and suggests that the figure was intended to be Greek. The
sole garment worn, or rather draped, around the youths,
is the Greek *chlamys* not the Roman *toga*. This Greek
atmosphere is further enhanced by the presence of the
elaborate *lyra* and the pair of *auloi*, both typically Greek
musical instruments. Neither was for the amateur: both
required considerable training. The eleven-stringed *lyra*
(see fig. 7), indeed, seems to have been invented in Greece
as a virtuoso instrument soon after 450 BC – it was part of
a new movement in music and is mentioned by the poet Ion
of Chios. Finally, the loose, long lock over the nape of the
boy's neck (fig. 31), which is also to be seen on the cameo

51

glass flask in a Swiss collection (see fig. 23, left) and in some of the representations on Arretine pottery (see fig. 25), was a Greek fashion, not a Roman one. Greek boys kept part of their hair long until reaching maturity, when they cut it off and offered it to the gods as part of the ritual transition to manhood. This rite, called the *koureion*, coincided with their acceptance into the citizen body, and happened between the ages of sixteen and eighteen. The long lock of hair indicates, therefore, that the boy is a citizen not a slave, as has sometimes been claimed. Representations of such special loose long locks in art begin to appear around the middle of the second century BC. Their braiding on the youth may have been the custom for older boys, perhaps after puberty was reached.

In conclusion, all the iconographical indicators, where they are specific, point away from a scene in a brothel (*lupanar*) that employed boys and youths, as well as women and girls, because we see citizen couples rather than slaves servicing citizens; they also point towards a Greek rather than a Roman setting. Is this simply because the artist was of Greek origin working in Greece or a Greek city? Or is it because he wished to create a Greek fantasy for a Roman clientèle? To attempt to answer such questions and to discover the cup's degree of Romanness, we need to look more closely at ancient Greek and Roman sexual customs.

In the Roman period representations of sexual acts are found not only on luxury goods, such as the Warren Cup and cameo glass vessels, and on mid-range products such as Arretine pottery, but also on much humbler terracotta lamps. Furthermore, they are to be seen on frescoes in places where nakedness and sexuality were apparently deemed acceptable: in bedrooms, in private houses and in changing rooms in public baths. Yet what precisely was acceptable to Roman society? From the extant literary sources, modern scholarship has identified a number of Roman sexual protocols, conceived by adult males and reinforcing the dominance of the male sex over the female, the free over the enslaved, and the adult over the young. The basic dividing line, it is argued, was between the active penetrator and the passive penetrated; that is, between

adult male citizens and the powerless sectors of society: women, boys and slaves. There was no division according to the gender of the partner, and so no concept of homosexuality and heterosexuality. This was a system that we would now define as being related to gender identity rather than sexual orientation. Nevertheless, there were some rules and these are well summed up in Plautus's play, *Curculio* (35–8), 'Love whatever you wish, as long as you stay away from married women, widows, virgins, young men and free boys.'

For those who stepped outside these parameters, if it was simply a matter of taking a passive role in sex – what a modern commentator might call sexuality slippage – they only did damage to their masculine identity (and were stigmatized as *cinnaedi* or *pathici*), whereas if they indulged in illicit sex with a freeborn female or male, they risked legal consequences. Unregulated sex with freeborn women was liable to lead to illegitimate children and thus conflicts over inheritance. This was something that society could not tolerate and in 18 BC Augustus introduced a law on adultery with severe penalties. Illicit sex with freeborn boys, however, was probably dealt with under the older, much less specific and rarely invoked *Lex Scantinia*, which covered all forms of sexual violations against freeborn Romans.

In ancient Greece, some of the same principles applied, but there were also differences, most notably in the existence of a well-established pederastic system that publicly acknowledged romantic and sexual mentor relationships between an adult male citizen (the *erastes*, or active lover) and a freeborn adolescent (the *eromenos*, or beloved) destined to become a citizen. Not all city-states would actually have shared the same code of male relationships: some, such as Sparta, Crete, Boeotia and Elis, officially sanctioned a pederastic system; others prohibited it outright. At Athens, where the visual evidence is most abundant and where nudity and sexual scenes are quite commonplace as decoration on pottery, we see that the picture was particularly complex. Representations of homoerotic courtship in sixth- and early fifth-century BC

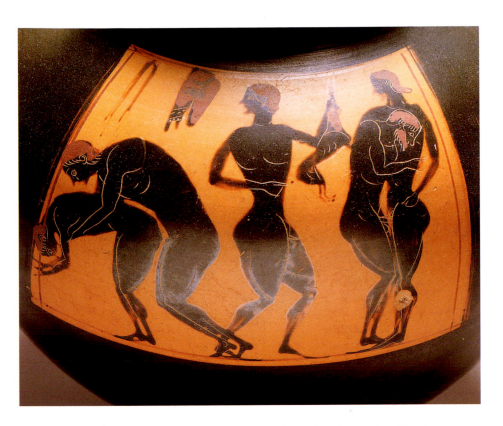

32 Athenian black-figured *hydria*, *c.* 510 BC (Collection of Leon Levy and Shelby White).

Athenian vase-painting show that it was ritualized as an 'honourable' versus 'shameful' process. The older *erastes* gained honour by success in his pursuit and shame by failure, while the younger *eromenos* won honour only in not openly succumbing and shame if he provided too much gratification. Here we find that when courtship has proved successful, often after the presentation of a gift – perhaps a garland, a toy or an animal – the *erastes* may touch the genitals of the *eromenos*, perhaps enjoy a kiss, and ultimately (fig. 32, right) be permitted to bow his head and bend his knees to move his penis between the thighs of the *eromenos* in what was called *diamerion* (nowadays referred to, somewhat inelegantly, as intracrural copulation). In all of this, the *eromenos* very rarely shows any emotion, except perhaps in the scenes of kissing, although occasionally an older *eromenos* may reveal an erection when *diamerion* is being performed. Most of the early examples of such scenes follow the pattern of a mature, bearded *erastes* with a youthful or boyish *eromenos*. There are, however, a number of exceptions where two youths are seen courting each other, or even two bearded men, while from the last decade of the sixth century onwards we find many more examples of youths courting boys. These scenes presumably reflect the fact that such relationships did not always come to an end once the youth reached maturity but could be for life, as well as the growing custom that they were as often instigated by youths before they had grown full beards as by more mature men.

There are very few images on Athenian vases of anal sex between two males. Besides those on a small group of vases of the middle of the sixth century BC that present such scenes as socially extreme actions by setting them in orgiastic or acrobatic contexts, there is only one preserved example. This is a late sixth-century BC black-figured *hydria* (water jar) in a New York private collection (fig. 32, left) that deliberately matches intracrural copulation with anal penetration. On this remarkable piece, to the right of the central *eromenos*, who holds a hare he has just been given (unless he is holding it for one of his friends), we see a bearded man bowed before a passive youth, indulging in *diamerion*. On the left, however, a youth penetrates another youth from behind. We should note perhaps that there is nothing obviously judgemental in this representation, rather both actions seem to be portrayed as equally acceptable.

Scenes of ritualized male courtship are very rarely seen on Athenian vases after about 470 BC. It may be that the increasingly radical democracy of fifth-century BC Athens marginalized the old aristocratic sexual values and customs of the sixth century. Such a change is perhaps also apparent in contemporary literature, especially late fifth-century BC comedy in which such behaviour is ridiculed. One vase from this period, however, stands out as exceptional. On this red-figured *krater* (bowl for mixing wine and water) in the British Museum a youth prepares to joyfully mount the lap of a second, slightly older seated youth (fig. 33). This takes place under the gaze of an older, bearded companion and

33 Athenian red-figured
krater, *c.* 420–410 BC
(British Museum).

a woman who peers out from over the top half of a door
which she has opened inwards. This scene has been
compared with representations of the myth behind the
second day of the Athenian wine festival, the Anthesteria,
due to the unusually large ribbons with additional
projections worn by the male figures and the cast of
characters itself. On this day Dionysos, the god of wine,
together with a couple of his satyrs visited the house of the
basilinna ('queen'; wife of the Archon Basileus, the leading
religious figure of the city). The painter may thus be
representing a comedy that made fun of the events of the
festival by turning Dionysos into a man (perhaps cast as
the priest of Dionysos) and his satyr companions into a
pair of frisky youths, while the *basilinna* (wife of the
Archon Basileus) watches from the door. According to such
a reading of what is an intriguing scene, the adoption of
a wildly festive context enabled the comic writer and the

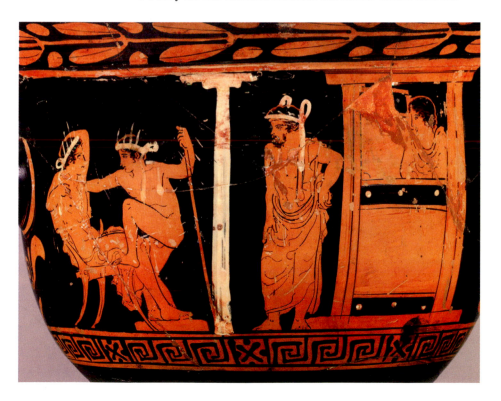

vase-painter to represent what otherwise might have been felt to be problematic.

In the Platonic dialogues of the first half of the fourth century BC a growing intellectualization of pederasty as chaste and spiritual is apparent, until in the *Laws*, Plato's last work, it is dismissed as unnecessary and unnatural. Pederasty, however, did not disappear in Athens but it clearly became deinstitutionalized and covert. Outside Athens the lack of visual evidence makes it very difficult to judge if there were similar changes elsewhere in the Greek world. Nevertheless, we know that a pederastic system continued in Sparta, Crete and Thebes into the Hellenistic period; and we may suppose that the Romans learnt of it mostly from the Greeks, although there remains a possibility that such a system was also known amongst some Italic peoples. In the cosmopolitan, Hellenistic world of the third and second centuries BC we seem to see a wider variety of poses and permutations in sex scenes, including a number of representations of penetrative male lovemaking. There is also perhaps a greater sense of intimacy between those involved, male and female, penetrator and penetrated, usually indicated by more kissing and tender caresses.

To return now to the scenes on the Roman Warren Cup, they show us, on one side, a bearded adult Greek penetrating a Greek youth who is at the upper end of what was called the *flos aetatis* (flower of life), the period between about thirteen and eighteen. On the other side is a slightly younger youth who has not yet dedicated his hair (perhaps sixteen years old) penetrating a boy on the threshold of puberty (perhaps twelve or thirteen; he is shown without pubic hair, which according to Aristotle grows at fourteen; at Sparta boys began to receive the attention of *erastai* at the age of twelve): both, as indicated by their hair, are Greeks of the citizen class. This sequencing of the ages of the participants is clear and deliberate, and, therefore, presumably significant.

We are certainly seeing something more subtle and complex than a visual equivalent to the lines of Strato, a second-century AD Roman poet, which describe the increasing degrees of pleasure to be got from boys for each year between twelve and seventeen, ending with the comment that 'if, however, one has a passion for those still older, he no longer "plays" but forthwith "receives his reply"'. This last description, however, might be connected with the difference between the two sides of the Warren Cup, for the partnership on the front is no longer simply active and passive, but both are now active.

Instead, what we are perhaps being shown, through the eyes of the Roman slave in the doorway, is a Greek pederastic scene, reflecting a system that might have been known to, or imagined by, the Romans of the first centuries BC and AD. It was not a system like the one created in sixth-century BC Athens where it would seem that an attempt was made to protect younger boys from anal sex, but rather one that allowed for fully physical relationships from even before puberty (as in Sparta and Crete). In Rome, although there is no evidence that a pederastic system was ever officially sanctioned, a pederastic ideal was not perhaps totally frowned upon, perhaps as part of a growing idealization of Greek culture. Even in Virgil's great, politically correct epic, the *Aeneid*, two pairs of Trojan heroes – Nisus and Euryalus, and Cydon and Clytius – are both represented as *erastes* and *eromenos*. Cydon is depicted fairly superficially as having 'constant love affairs with young men', but Nisus and Euryalus are drawn more fully, using terms such as 'devoted love' and 'shared love'. Indeed, as the latter are joined in death they emerge not only as having had the sort of bond that linked the warriors of the Theban Sacred Band in fourth-century BC Greece, but also both as being men of virtue.

At a *convivium* for which the Warren Cup was brought out, we can imagine the host enjoying faltering attempts, similar to our own, to decode its scenes, as well as the sort of ribald jokes that are always engendered by representations of sex. He might also have hoped for a serious discussion on contemporary and past morals, even if such talk never actually reached the heights of Plato's *Symposium*.

Chapter Seven
Conclusion

The Warren Cup has introduced us to some of the
complexities surrounding the understanding of sexuality
in antiquity, while its modern fate has pointed up some of
the ways in which attitudes to sexuality have changed over
the last century. This change is also visible in attitudes
to the display of objects such as the Warren Cup in the
British Museum and elsewhere. It was, in fact, the early
archaeological discoveries at Pompeii and Herculaneum
that, as they embarrassed and even shocked their finders,
began to lead to a suppression of erotic objects. As sexual
prudery increased, the pressure for secrecy grew and in
1820 all the offensive objects in the Herculaneum Museum
were removed to a separate room not open to the general
public, a 'Cabinet of Obscene Objects', which contained
some 200 'abominable monuments to human licentiousness'.

In Britain, too, a growing educated middle class began
to express its disapproval of both aristocratic corruption
and lower-class lack of values. By the late 1830s the British
Museum began to segregate some objects from various
cultures, including the Classical world. The formal creation
of its own 'Secretum' was eventually precipitated by the
donation in 1865 of 434 'Symbols of the Early Worship
of Mankind' by Dr George Witt. He hoped that 'some small
room may be appointed for its reception in which may also
be deposited and arranged the important specimens,
already in the vaults of the Museum – and elsewhere, which
are illustrative of the same subject'. This development was
itself in part prompted by the passing of the Obscene
Publications Act of 1857, for it seems likely that Witt
realized that upon his death his family might encounter
difficulties over the nature of his collection.

The British Museum's 'Secretum' eventually contained
as many as a thousand objects of a 'pornographic' nature,
including the six-layered cameo glass fragment with the
youth and the boy (see figs 34 and 24). Although attitudes

began to change in the first decades of the twentieth century objects continued to be added to the 'Secretum' until 1953 – the last objects to enter the collection were a number of late eighteenth-century condoms made from animal membrane and supplied with silk ribbons. Thereafter, the collection was dispersed throughout the Museum along cultural and chronological lines. Despite these changes, the time was not quite right for the purchase of the Warren Cup when it was first offered to the British Museum. By 1999, however, when the Museum had its second chance, society had perhaps reached a greater understanding and tolerance of both ancient and modern sexuality, and the cup could be displayed as a central object in the Museum's main Roman gallery.

Throughout history many societies, religions and power groups have sought to impose their own parameters for sexual behaviour with a variety of intentions, but most often as a means of preserving themselves. Some have violently turned against homosexuality in particular, including Christian fanatics – whether in Spain during the Inquisition or elsewhere in medieval Europe – and strict Jews, whose members in the vicinity of Jerusalem, where the Warren Cup had been hidden, would no doubt have wished to melt it down if they had ever seen it. Other cultures, however, have accepted passion between males, even celebrated it, such as in Han Dynasty China or pre-Meiji Japan.

The Warren Cup has led us down many paths, along which we have glimpsed, rather like its peeping slave, the diverse attitudes to representations of sexual acts of different societies over two thousand years. We have also tried to understand something of the cup's maker and his environment, as well as its several historical contexts, including its burial just outside Jerusalem at a time of great religious upheaval. While we continue to ponder all of these issues, especially those surrounding the meaning of the scenes on the cup, we should not lose sight of the extraordinary beauty and consummate artistry of this singular masterpiece of Roman art.

Photographic credits

All photographs copyright The Trustees of the British Museum, courtesy of the Department of Photography and Imaging, except for the following figs:

1   The Sunday Times News International, and Nick Newman
10 From Burdett and Goddard (photo Edward Reeves)
11 From Burdett and Goddard (photo Edward Reeves)
12 Lewes House, Lewes County Council, Lewes
13 Museum of Fine Arts, Boston (inv. 10.70, Gift of Nathaniel Thayer)
14 David Pardoe and Charleston Trust, Charleston House
15 Courtauld Institute, London (P.1947.LF.77)
16 Lewes House, Lewes County Council, Lewes
18 Musée du Louvre, Paris (Bj 1603)
19 National Museum, Copenhagen (inv. 9.20)
23 Collection of George Ortiz, Vandoeuvres
25 Museum of Fine Arts, Boston (inv. 13.109, Gift of E.P. Warren)
32 Collection of Leon Levy and Shelby White, New York

Details of British Museum objects:
2–9 and 30–31:
    GR 1999. 4-26.1
    (ht 11.0 cm; diam. at rim 11.0 cm)
17 and 29:
    GR 1960.2-1.2 and 3
    (ht 9.0 cm; diam. 9.9 cm)
20–21 and 26:
    GR 1960.2-1.1
    (ht 9.8 cm; diam. 12.5 cm)
22 GR 1840.12-5.41 and GR 1859.2-16.1
    (restored ht with handle 22.8 cm)
24 GR 1956.3-1.5 (width 4.9 cm)
27 GR 1867.5-8.1410; Catalogue of Silver 82 (diam. 14.7 cm)
28 GR 1999. 4-26.1
    (ht 11.0 cm; diam. at rim 11.0 cm)
29 GR 1850.3-4.35; Catalogue of Sculptures 1890 (ht 40.5 cm)
33 GR 1772.3-20.154; Catalogue of Vases F 65 (diam. at rim 32.5 cm)
34 Transferred from the Dept of Manuscripts to the Museum Secretum in 1891 (13 x 18 cm)

Further reading

F. Baratte, *Le Trésor d'Orfèvrerie romaine de Boscoreale* (Éditions de la Réunion des musées nationaux, Paris 1986).

Osbert Burdett and E.H. Goddard, *Edward Perry Warren: The Biography of a Connoisseur* (Christophers, London, 1941).

John R. Clarke, 'The Warren Cup and the contexts for representations of male-to-male lovemaking in Augustan and early Julio-Claudian art', *Art Bulletin* 75 (1993), 275–94.

John R. Clarke, *Looking at Lovemaking: Constructions of Sexuality in Roman Art 100 B.C.–A.D. 250* (University of California Press, Berkeley, 1998).

Kenneth J. Dover, *Greek Homosexuality* (2nd edn, MJF Books, New York, 1989).

Katherine M.D. Dunbabin, *The Roman Banquet: Images of Conviviality* (Cambridge University Press, Cambridge, 2003).

Donald B. Harden et al., *Glass of the Caesars* (Olivetti, Milan, 1987).

Thomas K. Hubbard (ed.), *Greek Love Reconsidered* (Wallace Hamilton Press, New York, 2000).

Catherine Johns, *Sex or Symbol? Erotic Images of Greece and Rome* (British Museum Press, London, 1982).

Kenneth S. Painter, *The Insula of the Menander at Pompeii. Volume IV: The Silver Treasure* (Oxford University Press, Oxford, 2001).

Lucia Pirzio Biroli Stefanelli, *L'Argento dei Romani: Vasellame da Tavola e d'Apparto* ('L'Erma' di Bretschneider, Rome, 1991).

John Pollini, 'The Warren Cup: Homoerotic Love and Symposium Rhetoric in Silver', *Art Bulletin* 81 (1999), 21–52.

Marilyn B. Skinner, *Sexuality in Greek and Roman Culture* (Blackwell, Oxford, 2005).

David Sox, *Bachelors of Art: Edward Perry Warren and the Lewes House Brotherhood* (Fourth Estate, London, 1991).

Donald E. Strong, *Greek and Roman Gold and Silver Plate* (Methuen, London, 1966).

Cornelius Vermeule, 'Augustan and Julio-Claudian court silver', *Antike Kunst* 6 (1963), 33–40.

David Whitehouse, 'Cameo Glass' in Martine Newby and Kenneth Painter (eds), *Roman Glass: Two Centuries of Art and Invention* (The Society of Antiquaries, London, 1991), 19–32.

Craig A. Williams, *Roman Homosexuality: Ideologies of Masculinity in Classical Antiquity* (Oxford University Press, Oxford, 1999).